Everything You Need to Know About

SEXUAL HARASSMENT

A woman might feel harassed by unwanted comments and stares.

• THE NEED TO KNOW LIBRARY •

Everything You Need to Know About

SEXUAL HARASSMENT

Elizabeth Bouchard

Series Editor: Evan Stark, Ph.D.

THE ROSEN PUBLISHING GROUP, INC.
NEW YORK

Published in 1990, 1992 by The Rosen Publishing Group, Inc.
29 East 21st Street, New York City, New York 10010

Revised Edition, 1992
Copyright © 1990, 1992 by The Rosen Publishing Group, Inc.

Manufactured in the United States of America.

Library of Congress Cataloging-in-Publication Data

Bouchard, Elizabeth.
  Everything you need to know about sexual harassment / Elizabeth Bouchard. —Revised ed.
  (The Need to know library)
  Includes bibliographical references and index.
  Summary: Discusses how to recognize and deal with sexual harassment and where to go for help.
  ISBN 0-8239-1490-9
  1. Sexual harassment—United States—Prevention—Juvenile literature. [1. Sexual harassment.] I. Title. II. Title: Sexual harassment. III. Series.
HQ72.U53B68   1990
305.3—dc20   89-39508
                                                                  CIP
                                                                   AC

Contents

Introduction

Have you ever gotten a funny feeling when your boss watches you work? Maybe he stares too much. Maybe he says things that seem nice, but make you uncomfortable. Maybe he asks a lot of questions about your boyfriends. Maybe he touches or nudges you for no good reason.

Have you ever been in a class with a teacher who wants you to stay late for extra help, even though you understand the lesson well enough? Maybe the teacher wants to spend more time "getting to know you." Maybe she/he flatters you by telling you how mature or attractive you are. Maybe you really do need extra help. But your teacher lets you know that you'll need to do more than study with her or him to pass the course!

Both these situations describe forms of sexual harassment. Sexual harassment happens to all kinds of people in all kinds of places. It happens to men as well as to women. It happens in offices, classrooms, on the street, and in social settings. One of the worst things about sexual harassment is the way it can make you feel: scared, confused, embarassed, angry, and powerless. Any time someone makes you feel threatened sexually they are harassing you. They may do it by making inappropriate remarks, teasing, touching, asking for favors or promising favors. When someone tries to force you to accept this treatment so that you can keep your job or get a passing grade in a class, they are also breaking the law.

What should you do if you are being sexually harassed? Where can you go for help? What rights do you have and how can you protect yourself? This book will help you find answers to these questions. It will also help you understand what sexual harassment is and some of the many reasons it happens.

If you are in a situation like this, you already know how hard it can be to handle. But understanding sexual harassment will help you to deal with your feelings. Knowing the facts can help you to find some solutions. It may even help you avoid harassment in the future.

Sexual comments that are meant to embarrass someone are a form of sexual harassment.

Chapter 1

Real Life Situations

In a Group

For Sharon, the job training program was a new beginning. She had not been able to get work since she had dropped out of high school. She hoped the training program would teach her job skills. She also planned to study for her high school equivalency diploma at the same time.

Celia was the only other girl in her training group. Sharon didn't mind. She just wanted to have a job. For a while she didn't listen to the way the trainer talked about her and Celia. He would say things to the whole group, things like, "Females have to learn to do something besides lie down." Or "You won't get along here by shakin' your bootie." He seemed to think that because they were women they were lazy.

Some of the guys in the training group picked up the trainer's way of thinking and talking. Every day someone would say something about Sharon's body, or Celia's. One day Sharon found a picture of a naked woman pasted to her locker door. Finally, Celia was so upset that she quit. Sharon felt really alone. She couldn't think in class. She wanted to tell somebody what was happening. But no one had actually laid a hand on her. So she felt there was nothing she could do.

You Decide

What do you know about sexual harassment? Do you think that Sharon's rights have been violated? Is there anything she can do?

Answer these questions to see if you agree with the experts.

1. The guys were probably only joking around. She should not have listened to the comments.
   True ?
   False ?
2. Females ask for this because they expect special treatment.
   True ?
   False ?
3. Sharon's problem is not sexual harassment. She was never touched, propositioned or threatened.

True ?
False ?
4. There is nothing Sharon could do but quit, like Celia.
True ?
False ?

ANSWERS

1. False. This kind of talk was *hostile*. It was done to embarass Sharon and Celia. The trainer was saying that Sharon and Celia were not as good as he and the other guys. Probably the attacks would not stop if Sharon ignored them.

2. False. This is the way the trainer thinks. Judging people by sex or race or religion makes it impossible for women to be treated as equals. Even if one woman did exchange sexual favors for special treatment, this does not mean that all women do. This kind of thinking is the way some men say it's O.K. to expect special treatment for men.

3. False. One does not have to be physically assaulted, propositioned or threatened. To harass someone is to torment them. *Sexual comments, looks or gestures* are also sexual harassment. They are meant to embarrass someone.

4. False. Sexual harassment is illegal. It violates a person's civil rights. For a discussion of what Sharon can do, go to Chapter 6.

In the Classroom

Vanessa was a junior in a big city high school. She sang in the choir. She was a pretty good student. She and some of her friends were going to try out for the school play. It was going to be a good year, except for one thing: biology.

Biology was a hard class. You had to memorize a lot of terms. You had to find cells under a microscope. You had to cut up creepy things, like worms. Vanessa knew she was going to hate it.

The biology teacher was also the coach of the boys' basketball team. He was popular with the students. He didn't stand at the front of the class and lecture. Instead, he gave students projects to do on their own each day. If you didn't understand something, you could go to him for help.

Looking back, Vanessa knows now that she could easily have passed the course. But at the time she had a bad attitude. She was sure she couldn't learn biology. She failed the first test. Before the next test, she took her workbook to the teacher. They stood by the bookshelves next to the window. He guided her hand, and helped her redraw one of her diagrams. He explained terms to her. Then he quizzed her on them—while standing arm to arm with her. Later, he told her she didn't have to take the next quiz. He was sure that she knew the material.

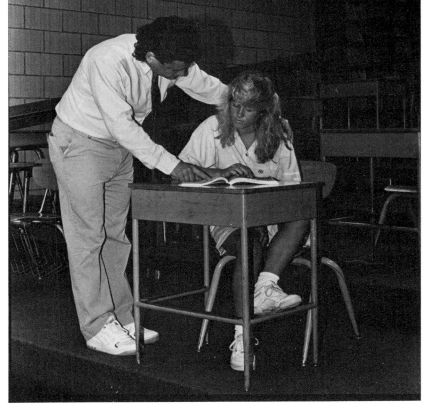

A teacher may try to get too friendly while helping a student.

Vanessa was happy. She hated studying alone. And she was pleased by the teacher's interest in her. He was a popular teacher, and a coach. If he liked her, she must be all right.

The next week her teacher asked her to go with him after school. He had to pick up some supplies for the basketball team. He wanted the boys to practice, he said. He could talk to her about biology on the way there.

They didn't talk about biology. They stopped to have a hamburger. Before she knew it, Vanessa was in the back seat of the car with her teacher.

For a while, Vanessa felt OK about her special relationship. The other students said things about

her. But she knew they were just jealous. Best
of all, she didn't have to study biology anymore.
She got an A in the course on every report card.

But the next semester Vanessa had another
biology teacher. She didn't understand what was
going on in class. She had not had to learn
anything in her first semester class. She asked the
coach for help, but he seemed to be too busy. He
stopped taking her out after school. One day
Vanessa waited for him after school. She saw him
go out to his car with another girl student.

Vanessa got very depressed. She knew she would
fail biology. She felt that her teacher/boyfriend had
used her. He had not really cared for her. The girls
teased her about him. "Where is your boyfriend,
Vanessa?" they called. "Maybe you weren't smart
enough for him!" And with a bad grade average
she would not be able to be in the school play.
Her future at school looked dark. Vanessa stopped
going to school regularly. Then she decided to
drop out completely.

You Decide

You already know a lot about people and life. You
can see Vanessa's story more clearly than she
could. You can look at her situation clearly because
you are not involved.

Answer these questions to see if you agree with
the experts.

1. Vanessa was tricked into the teacher's sexual abuse because:
   a. She was young and didn't know better.
   b. She felt unable to keep up in the biology class.
   c. She did not want to face a hard course without help.
   d. All of the above.
2. Vanessa had no real choice in the beginning: She could either fail the course or go along with the teacher.
   a. True ?
   b. False ?
3. Since she made a mistake, Vanessa should drop out of school and give up.
   a. True ?
   b. False ?

ANSWERS

1. (d) Studies show that the victims of sexual harassment are usually *young and inexperienced.* They feel they have no power. Victims also often have low *self-esteem.* They are unsure of themselves. For more about victims of harassment, see Chapter 4.
2. (b) Vanessa had several choices. Remember, it is the teacher's job to help students learn. No other payment is necessary. Vanessa could have gone to a counselor for help. She could have asked for tutoring. She also could have studied with friends.

3. (b) That is the once-a-victim, always-a-victim
way of thinking. Vanessa should talk to a
counselor or teacher. There are many ways she
can improve her grades. Dropping out will only
make her bad self-image worse. It will make her
an easy victim of other kinds of abuse.

On the Job

Richie was a whiz in English. In fact, he liked to
read. After school he usually stopped off at the
library. He always kept an adventure book he was
reading on a library shelf. It was hidden behind
some other books. That way he wouldn't have to
take it home.

Home was a problem for Richie. He, his mother
and his four little brothers and sisters lived in a
small apartment. It was always noisy and crowded.
It was not a good place for reading. He was the
oldest. His mother expected him to watch out for
the little ones. She always had hot food on the
table, though. She kept things as clean as she
could. His father lived somewhere else. Richie
didn't see him very often.

One day Hector asked him if he wanted an
afternoon job. Hector was in Richie's gym class.
Richie said sure. Jobs that paid well were hard to
find. He could use the money to buy himself a
cassette player. Maybe he would buy a present for
his mom.

The next week Richie went with Hector to the warehouse where he was going to work. The boss, Mr. B., was an older guy, but friendly. He told Richie what the work schedule and the pay would be. He then told Hector to show Richie how to load boxes on the dolly and where to move them.

Richie was happy with the job. He enjoyed hanging out with the other guys. Having a job made him feel like a man. He also didn't have to ask his mother for money anymore. So she didn't mind so much that he wasn't home to help with the little kids.

The guys at work were always joking around. They liked arm-wrestling, seeing who could pick up the heaviest box, things like that. The boss didn't seem to mind. In fact, one afternoon he said he would hold a contest. He wanted to see who had the best-looking muscles.

A boss has no right to demand a personal relationship.

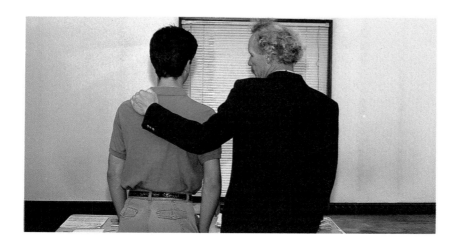

The boss brought a camera. Richie and the other two guys had to strip down to their underwear. They had to pose in front of the boxes. Mr. B. told Richie he looked real nice, even though he was the smallest one. Richie felt good about that. He was grateful to Mr. B. for helping him out. He was glad to have a job.

One evening, just as they were leaving, Mr. B. called Richie in the office. When the others had gone, he put his arm around Richie's shoulders. He told Richie that he was a smart kid. He said he wanted to help Richie get ahead in life. But, he added, business was slow. He would have to let Richie go.

Unless, of course, Richie wanted to have a "personal relationship."

Richie was confused. He now depended on the job. The money let him help his mom. He was also grateful to the boss for his help. He didn't usually get a lot of attention. But Richie also knew what a "personal relationship" meant. He didn't want that kind of relationship. He wanted a friend. He couldn't take his problem to Hector and the guys. They would laugh and call him a "sissy." His mother would go crazy. He felt completely alone.

You Decide

Did Richie do anything to get in this jam? What should he do now? See if your answers about

Richie's problem are the same as what the experts think.

1. Richie is in trouble because:
   a. He must really be a "sissy."
   b. He is young and innocent.
   c. He needs money.
2. Richie ought to:
   a. Stick it out, since he needs the money.
   b. Quit, because he could mess up his life.
   c. See if he can keep the job without the sex stuff.

ANSWERS

1. (b) People often want to *blame the victim* for the crime. Richie is not at fault because his boss is attracted to him. Mr. B.'s offer does not mean that Richie is a homosexual. Being poor is not a crime, either. Millions of school kids have part-time jobs to help out their family or earn spending money. Mr. B. is the problem. He is taking advantage of Richie's youth and innocence.

2. (b) Mr. B. is really *blackmailing* Richie. First he fires him, then offers Richie his job back if he will go along. Richie will not be able to keep the job without the sexual favors. If he does go along, things will only get worse. He will be more isolated. Mr. B is not a friend. He is taking advantage of Richie. For a better understanding of a harasser like Mr. B., see Chapter 3.

Unwanted touching by a fellow worker is harassment.

Chapter 2

How to Spot Sexual Harassment

There is no need to feel alone if you have been the victim of sexual harassment on the job. In a recent survey by a large women's magazine, 88% of women responding said they had been sexually harassed at work.

It is clear that sexual harassment is a problem.

But what exactly is sexual harassment? What's the difference between a friendly compliment, or a supportive hug, and harassment? The difference is simple. Any *unwanted* or *inappropriate* sexual attention is sexual harassment. That includes touching, looks, comments, or gestures. Sexual harassment usually happens in situations where one person (the harasser) has more power or authority than another person (the victim). Sexual harassment can happen anywhere. Doctors can harass patients. Teachers can harass students. Bosses can harass employees. Customers in a restaurant can even harass waiters and waitresses.

Whenever, wherever, and however sexual harassment happens, it is always unpleasant. It may be humiliating and frightening. It may even be dangerous. Sexual harassment may make you worry about losing your job. Or you may be afraid for your personal safety.

For a better understanding of what sexual harassment *is*, let's take a look at *what it is not*.

1. It is *not* the victim's fault.
2. It is *not* just harmless fun or flirtation.
3. It is *not* normal sexual attraction.
4. It is *not* just something made up by men and women who are cold, unfriendly, or no fun.
5. Women *do not* "ask for it" by being attractive or pretty. (Neither do men.)

It is One-sided and Unwelcome

A key part of sexual harassment is that it is one-sided and unwelcome. This is not romance or friendship. Those feelings are shared by two people.

When someone insists that you accept their sexual attention, even if you are not interested, they are sexually harassing you. You are not responsible for their bad behavior. They have a problem. Their actions are inappropriate, abusive and wrong. Their actions are against the law. Unfortunately, sexual harassment often makes the victim feel guilty. *Remember, it is not your fault!* The person who forces unwanted sexual attention is to blame.

It's About Power

Fear is often part of sexual harassment. That is because sexual harassment is not about physical attraction. *It is about power.* Some people just like power over others. They like to see that they are feared. They enjoy making people do things for them.

On the job, a supervisor may give you a hard time. He may let you know that the only way for you to keep your job or to get ahead is to give him sexual favors. At school, a teacher may promise a good grade or a place on a team if you "go along."

If you are the only female or male in your work area, it may be a problem. The others may harass you to "keep you in your place." Almost always, the offender wants to make you afraid.

It Happens Over and Over

Sexual harassment almost always *happens over and over.* The offensive gesture, invitation or action is repeated again and again. Every time you go to the water cooler, he's blocking your way. At first you ignore it. But it keeps happening. You feel tense and upset. You dread going to work. You find excuses not to go.

It Seems to Get Worse

Often, the more you try to avoid harassment, the worse the problem gets. You may find reasons to stay away from the harasser but he may begin to bother you even more. If you fight back a little, he may want to scare you. The only defense is to be firm. Tell him to leave you alone. Try not to show how upset you are. And always get help. Any kind of sexual harassment is against the law.

Examples

Sexual remarks, teasing and jokes are common at work. They may seem to be spoken "in fun." But they are not fun to the victim. Remarks like, "Hey, baby, what's your statistics" and "Get a load of those buns" make a person feel cheapened. Debra, an office messenger, had this complaint:

> *Every time my boss asks me to do something, he says something like, "I know you can convince Mr. So and So to do this. Just flutter your eyelashes at him." Or "It will be easy to get him to sign this now. Just lean over his desk and let him get a good look." I try to ignore him.*

Suggestive looks and gestures are another way of bothering someone. Staring or leering are aggressive ways of showing sexual interest. Sandra's boss would never look her in the eye. He stared at her breasts when he talked to her. He kept his hands in his pockets all the time, as if he was rubbing his penis.

Demands for dates and sexual favors from a co-worker or a supervisor are types of harassment.

Often these are accompanied by threats, like "If
you want to get along, you go along." New people
on the job are very easy targets for this kind of
threat. Sometimes an old-timer or a supervisor will
promise special favors. Captain Creep promises you
an easy assignment if you put out. The manager
says he will let you move to the day shift if you go
out with him. These are not favors. They are
threats. They show the power of the abuser and the
lack of power of the victim.

Touching and other kinds of physical contact
can be unpleasant and frightening. One high school
gym teacher liked to put his arm around the girls
and push up against them. He did this when he
showed how to hold a tennis racket. A hospital lab
worker complained that a co-worker embarrassed
her. He would come up and give her a back-rub
while she was working. No one has the right to
touch you *in any way*, ever, unless you say it is
okay. Unwanted touching is not friendly. It is rude
and unacceptable. You always have the right to tell
a person not to touch you, no matter who it is.
Your body is yours to control.

Remember these points about sexual harassment:

○ Sexual harassment is one-sided and unwelcome.
○ It is about power and not about attraction.
○ It happens over and over again.
○ It gets worse.

Bullies need victims. They pick on people who are weaker.

Chapter 3

Why Does It Happen?

Being aware of certain types of behavior may help you to recognize a harasser. It puts you on guard. It may help you know when you can help yourself or when you should go for help.

Remember that sexual harassment is about power. Harassers are people who need to bully others, in order to feel powerful. They like to push other people around. Making fun of other people makes them feel important. They like to make other people feel afraid.

Let's look at some of the different types of harassers.

The Bully

Bullies need victims and are good at finding them. They pick on the people who are weaker. They pick on the ones they think won't defend themselves. You see, bullies are really cowards. They may have been victims themselves. They probably have a bad self-image. Having power over others makes them feel better about themselves.

Bullies like to use power to push other people around. Bullies are sometimes foremen or supervisors. Sometimes they have been around a long time and they know how the system works. They may be older. They may be friends with the boss.

Bullies are sometimes like gangsters: they have their own turf. They "run" a certain section of the floor, a certain part of the plant. They don't want other people moving in. They don't want females "doing a man's job." Or they don't want men "messing up women's work."

Since bullies are cowards, sometimes you can beat them just by standing up to them.

The Egotist

A person who will do anything to have something his own way is an egotist. An egotist will run over anyone who gets between him and what he wants. She will also use anyone to get what she wants.

Egotists are fairly easy to shake off. Let them know you are on to their game and are not interested. They will try to find other victims.

Macho Man and the Tramp

These types of personalities don't relate to others in a real way. Their behavior is like playacting. When imitating a movie star or TV character, they think they have the right to treat other people badly. Acting rough and tough or very sexy can make them feel more important and attractive. This kind of person is called a *fantasist*. A fantasist lives in a make-believe world and wants others to play along.

The Sadist

Sadists like to cause other people pain. It gives them pleasure. They may have been abused as children. They have learned that power can be used to hurt and embarass others. Sexual harassment may be a way for them to hurt someone the way they have been hurt. Sadists are sick. Their minds are twisted. They can be very dangerous.

Bullies, egotists, fantasists and sadists often find protection in the work place. They also find their victims.

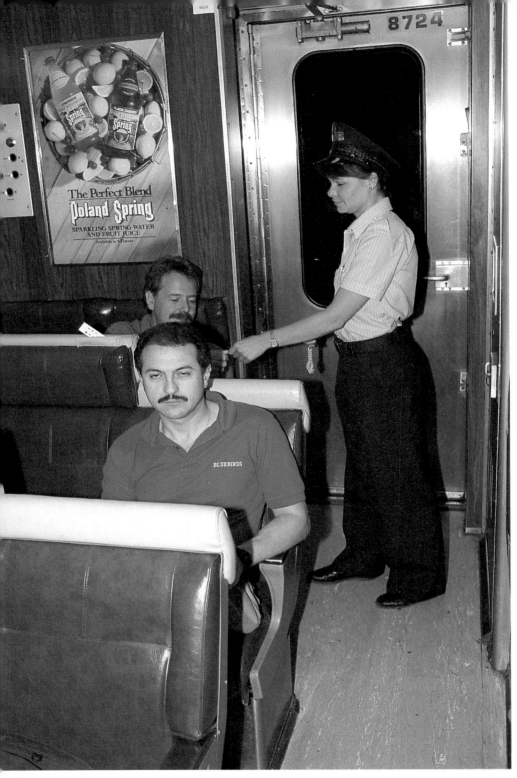

A woman should feel comfortable in doing a job that usually has been done only by men.

Chapter 4

Who Does It Happen To?

In situations where one person is in a position of power over another, sexual harassment can easily happen. Sexual harassment is found in many kinds of relationships. A doctor and patient, or teacher and student, are common examples. It can also be a problem for a boss and employee, a customer and salesperson, or even a coach and athlete. Any situation can become an opportunity for harassment. It depends on the two particular people involved.

Some people are more likely to be harassed than others. And some situations are more likely to lead to harassment. In this chapter you will learn more about the different kinds of victims of sexual harassment.

Men can also be victims of sexual harassment.

The New Kid on the Block

Any new situation with new people can put you at risk. Whether you are starting a job or starting school, you have a lot to learn. You will be eager to do a good job and make a good impression. It is hard to know at first when to agree and when to say no to things that are asked of you. For example: What if your boss asks you to stay late to talk about personal things? What if a teacher says that there are special after-hour study sessions you must attend? Because you are new you do not know the normal routine. The person in power may be taking advantage of you.

Be aware of your feelings. If you feel uncomfortable, there may be a good reason for it. Talk to someone you trust. Perhaps a fellow worker or student could help you to understand what is going on.

Special Problems Facing Women

In our society there are many people who do not respect women. Many men believe that it is okay to treat women only as sexual objects. They may tell themselves that this is what women *want* from men. They are wrong.

Most cases of sexual harassment happen to women who are abused by men. These women may have very low self-esteem. They may need to please others in order to feel good about themselves. But they are not alone. Sexual harassment can happen to anyone.

It is not always possible to avoid harassment. You are not responsible for someone else's behavior. But there may be some simple things you can do to stop harassment before it worsens. If a man on the street bothers you, cross the street. If you are sharing a seat with someone whose behavior is not acceptable, find a new seat. It is not always easy to speak up for yourself. And it takes courage to do new things. But it is important to try to discourage harassment as early as possible. These suggestions may help:

1. Don't accept a man's bad attitude toward women. If someone does not respect you, it is their problem. You can always respect yourself.

2. Think about the way you dress and how you act around men. What kind of attention are you looking for? What reaction are you getting?

3. Try not to be alone with anyone who makes you uncomfortable in any way. Make friends.

4. Be sure of yourself. Make your own decisions. You are less likely to be bothered by a harasser if you appear to be in control.

Men Have Trouble Too

Women are not the only victims of sexual harassment. More and more men are being harassed in the workplace, classrooms, and locker rooms. Whoever is in a position of power has the advantage. Men can be victims of male or female harassers.

Sexual harassment is always wrong. No one deserves it. The harasser is always to blame. And it is always hurtful to the victim.

Looking Like a Victim

Everyone knows that a bully is most likely to pick on someone who acts afraid. Harassers are bullies. They are quick to notice actions that they see as weaknesses. They will try to take advantage

1. **THE MARTYR.** This person is looking for ways to be hurt. She or he is always willing to give a little more than is necessary. Harassers know they can treat the martyr badly and never hear complaints.

2. **THE SHOW-OFF.** This person is trying hard to get attention, even if the attention is bad.

Some people cling to anyone in charge. They may try too hard to please them.

3. **THE OUTCAST.** This person doesn't fit in. He or she is probably very shy and self-conscious. He or she may prefer to be alone. It may be very hard for the outcast to make friends. The harasser knows this person is an easy victim because he or she has no one to turn to for help.

Sexual harassment is a common problem. But it can often be avoided or stopped. In the next chapter we will discuss ways you can help yourself not to become a victim.

Harassment may be avoided by keeping everything strictly on a business level.

Chapter 5

Avoiding Sexual Harassment

We have seen that sexual harassment is a common problem in many areas of our lives. Does that mean a person just has to endure sexual harassment, like the flu? Certainly not.

In some ways though, harassment is like the flu.

○ It indicates an unseen disease (although a social one).

○ It makes you feel awful.

○ It disrupts your life.

○ You cannot be certain of avoiding it.

But just because you are exposed to it doesn't mean you can't fight back. In the next chapter we will look at some actions to take to stop sexual harassment. But first, let's consider ways to *avoid* it

Ways of Avoiding Harassment

Probably the best way to avoid sexual harassment in the first place is to trust your instincts, or gut feelings. Usually they'll warn you that something is wrong with a person's behavior. Often we ignore those feelings and tell ourselves we're just imagining things or "over-reacting." Trust your feelings. They'll help keep you from falling into the harasser's trap.

Here are some things you can do to discourage a would-be harasser:

○ *Keep everything strictly on a business level.* Avoid lunches, after-hours meetings, even friendly chats. Avoid being alone with the harasser.

○ If you have to work in the same room as the harasser, create a barrier between you. Move your desk or a file cabinet.

○ Do not ask for *personal favors* or special treatment from the harasser. You do not want to owe the person anything.

○ Just say No! to any advances, right from the start.

○ Do not talk about anything *personal*. Keep your own life private. Don't listen to personal problems.

○ Be as strong and certain of yourself as you can. Don't let a harasser see your weak spots.

Four Reasons to Take Action

1. Victims need to protect themselves.

2. You may not be alone. Others are being hurt too.

3. Being sexually harassed is very unpleasant.

4. Sexual harassment is against the law.

Legal fees are expensive. Consult a lawyer only after you have tried all other ways to stop the harassment.

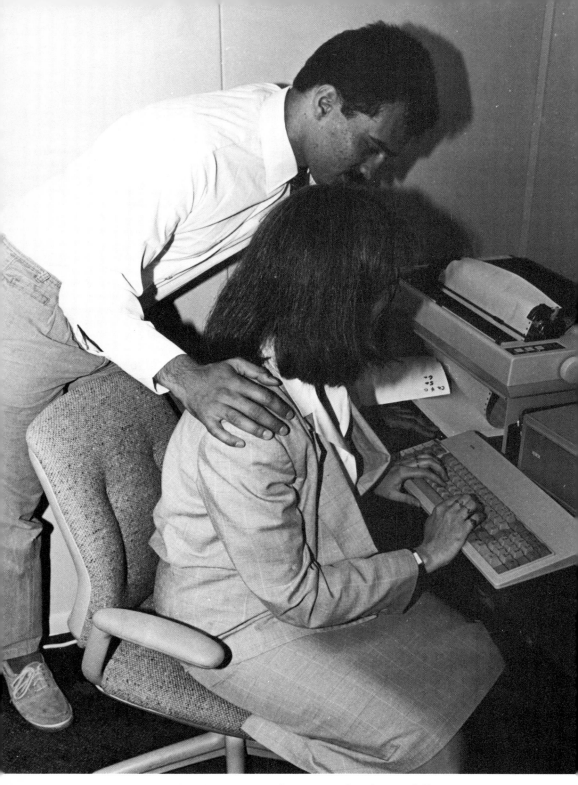

A boss or coworker should not touch or nuzzle close while explaining a task.

Chapter 6

Choices for Action

Usually the worst thing you can do is to ignore harassment. The offender may think you are playing the game. Or he may think that you are confused and about to give in. The offender may also think that you are not taking him or her seriously. That may make him angry, even violent. Giving in will damage your self-esteem. It will also give the offender power over you.

The best thing to do is to *help yourself*. Here are some of the things you can do.

1. Keep a Record.

Write notes when things happen, in case you have to make a complaint. It is easy to "forget" things that are unpleasant. If you keep careful notes, you do not have to think back to the incident. It is carefully recorded. You can keep a small notebook in your pocket for this purpose. You can even write on a napkin or matchbook to help you remember. Write down:

○ when it happened
○ where it happened
○ what time it happened
○ what actually took place and what the offender said
○ how you felt
○ the names of any witnesses

Here is a sample of what you might write.

Feb. 6, 1989—the stockroom—2:30 p.m.

Mr. Smith asked me to meet him. He wanted to show me how to mark some new merchandise. When I got there he put his arm around me, but I moved away. When he was showing me how to fill out the form, he said he liked my perfume. I didn't have any on. He wanted to talk about me. I said I had to get back to help Katie. I hate to be alone with him.

2. Confront the Person.

Have a talk with the harasser. *Take a friend along* with you. Talk about the times you were harassed. Tell him clearly what you object to. For instance,

instance, "You have put your arm around me several times. You have no right to touch me." Or, "You keep saying sexual things to me. They have nothing to do with work." Tell the harasser that you want him to stop. Tell him you will report him if he doesn't.

Another way to do this is to write a letter to the harasser. Be sure to keep a copy. Tell the person *clearly* in your letter that you do not like his or her behavior toward you. Tell the person that if you are not left alone, you will report it.

Why Write?

Writing a letter is a good idea. That way the person will have time to think it over calmly. The person is less likely to react angrily or violently. A letter also shows that you are serious. It shows you are able to think for yourself. It shows you can protect yourself.

Here is an example of this kind of letter.

> Dear Mr. Jones:
> Many times you have said things in front of people about my clothes and my looks. You keep saying sexual things to me when we are alone. These things upset me, and I am asking you to stop. I don't want to report this, but I will if you don't stop.

3. Talk to Someone in Charge.

If the letter does not stop the harassment, you have two choices. You must find a powerful friend. Or you can go directly to someone in charge who can put a stop to the problem. Let's look at the first choice: a powerful friend.

If you are under eighteen, then your parents can probably help you the most. If the trouble is at school, your mother and father can go to the principal with you. The same goes for work. Your parents have had more experience in the work world. They are less likely to be scared of the harasser. Remember, sexual harassment is a power play. Being young and inexperienced puts you at a disadvantage.

Sometimes parents can't help. Then you must go directly to someone with power. In a company, school or other organization, there may be a special office to deal with complaints about sexual harassment. If not, you may go to your boss, your teacher, or your superior officer. If one of them is the one who is harassing you, then you should go to *his* or *her* boss. In schools, there are often counselors you can talk to.

Before you talk to this person, *prepare yourself.* It is not easy to talk to another person about sexual harassment. You may feel frightened or embarrassed. You may get confused and "forget" what you had to say.

○ To prepare, use your notebook as your record. Write down a list of the things the person has done to harass you. Write down the bad effect this has had on you. When you report the problem, tell your story as calmly as you can.

A letter to the harasser may be a good way to stop the problem.

Use the details you have written down. These
will help the person in charge understand the
situation better.

○ Be prepared that the person may not believe you
at first. You may get disbelief: "But Mr. Smith
is such a friendly person. Are you sure you
aren't mistaken?"

○ Take a friend along to support you. A friend can
help you stay cool.

At Work, Go to Management

○ If your company has a formal way to make a
complaint, follow it. You will have to write out a
complaint. Your journal will help you. You will
certainly be given the chance to talk. If you can,
discuss this issue with a woman manager. She
probably has had experience with harassment.
She may be kinder and more understanding.
Companies are legally responsible for sexual
harassment on the job. Managers take
complaints seriously. Give your complaint in
writing.

○ Make a copy of anything you send.

○ Tell the person you complain to that you will
call them in a few days. Tell him you will want

to know what is being done. This way you can be sure that the company will act on the matter without delay.

Legal Actions

If your complaint to the management does not bring results, there are other things you can do. Sexual harassment is illegal. Victims of sexual harassment can make complaints to a number of government agencies. A victim can also hire a lawyer. She can sue the *employer* if the company does not act on a complaint of sexual harassment.

Before you call a lawyer, think about this:

○ Going through government agencies or the courts can take months, or even years. Be prepared for a long battle.

○ Hiring a lawyer is expensive. But you may be able to get a free consultation at a Legal Aid office.

○ If you are still at work, you may be put under a lot of pressure by the company. Your workplace may be unpleasant. Consider legal action as a last resort. Consider it when all other means have failed. Or consider it when you have been severely harmed. If you have been raped, or physically hurt, or the harassment has caused a serious problem in your life, take action.

JUDGING CLARENCE THOMAS

During the fall of 1991, the subject of sexual harassment grabbed news headlines. Everyone began discussing this issue. And emotions ran high.

Judge Clarence Thomas was nominated to be a Supreme Court justice. The Supreme Court is America's highest court. Supreme Court justices have their jobs for life. They cannot be fired. Before a person can be made a justice, he or she must be questioned and approved by Congress.

Judge Thomas was once the head of a U.S. agency called the EEOC. The EEOC makes sure everyone is treated fairly when applying for a job. It also enforces laws against sexual harassment.

Anita Hill is a law professor who worked with Judge Thomas at the EEOC many years ago. A few weeks into the Congressional questioning she came forward and accused Thomas of sexual harassment. She claimed that he used to constantly ask her for dates and spoke to her about pornographic films he had seen. Anita Hill said that she was deeply offended by these remarks but felt that she could not complain. Clarence Thomas was her boss and she thought that her career could be in trouble if she made a fuss.

Anita Hill was a very believable witness. But Judge Thomas denied her charges in the strongest possible terms.

Who was telling the truth? The country was divided. But the issue was being discussed everywhere. Women from all across the nation told of their experiences with sexual harassment. And many men admitted being insensitive to this issue.

Finally, the Senate voted to approve Judge Thomas. But the vote was close. Many senators had doubts about Thomas's character. Others did not think Thomas's career should be destroyed because of one person's story. They said there was not enough evidence to prove there was wrongdoing. In the end, everyone agreed that sexual harassment is a serious problem we all must become more sensitive to.

Government Agencies

Equal Employment Opportunity Commission (EEOC)—Sexual harassment is unlawful. It violates the Civil Rights Act of 1964. The EEOC has set rules about sexual harassment in the workplace. The EEOC will investigate and prosecute cases which meet its rules. That means the government will take your case to court.

In larger cities, you can find the number for the EEOC listed under United States Government in the telephone directory. If you do not have an agency office in your city, you can write the headquarters in Washington, D.C. At the end of this book, you will find a page of addresses.

Human Rights Commission—Each state has a department that checks out civil rights violations. You can find the number under "State of . . . (your state)" in the telephone directory.

Women's Organizations

Most of the victims of sexual harassment have been women. So many women's organizations can help you to deal with this problem. Women's organizations can often help you get in touch with people who can help you. See the list on page 60 for some names.

A victim may feel alone and full of self pity.

Chapter 7

How to Cope

As we said in the last chapter, there is a good reason to try to avoid harassment. Being harassed can make you feel so awful. But what if your best efforts haven't paid off?

It is very easy to be full of *self-pity* when you are a victim. "Everyone is against me," you groan. "I was born unlucky. Even God doesn't love me." And having these thoughts, you give up. Like Vanessa, you go limp. You drop out. You settle for whatever comes along. You see yourself as a permanent victim.

But there is a choice. You don't have to end up a loser. And since no one *has* to be a loser, why would anyone *want* to be? Not you, right? Good.

But your self-esteem, your normal pride in yourself, has taken a beating. You've got the blues. You're also feeling alone. To cope, learn how to strengthen and get back your self-esteem. Learn how to break out of your isolation.

How to Feel Better about Yourself

1. Brag about yourself. Take a nice, clean sheet of paper and list things that you like about yourself. You are down in the dumps now. But *look at yourself from the point of view of someone who knows and likes you.* See yourself as your mother, grandmother, friend, or teacher might see you.

Answer these questions:
o What can I do well?
o How do I treat other people?
o What good attitudes do I have?
o What special talents do I have?
o What is nice about my appearance?
o What dreams and goals do I have?
o What interests and activities do I have?
o What interesting personality traits do I have?
o What inner thoughts and feelings do I have?

Try to come up with two or three good things about yourself for each question. Don't sell yourself short. "I get places on time" may not be very exciting to you. But your boss, your teachers and your friends will rate this quality highly.

Read over your list. Select the ten good things that you rate most highly. Then rank them on how important they are. Take this list with you. Paste it on the bathroom mirror. Hang it next to your bed as a reminder. Every day look for chances to *show* these pluses to yourself and other people.

2. Make yourself in your best image. The closer you get to the way you want to be, the happier you will be. Begin by completing the following sentence in five ways:
"I would like myself much better if I were *more*

_____ ."

Now finish this sentence in five ways:
"I would like myself much better if I were *less*

_____ ."

You now have ten points that describe your ideal. Your goal is not to become your ideal. That is never possible. But you can come closer to it.

3. Act as if you were . . . . What if you said you would like yourself better if you were more confident. What do you mean by confident? If you were self-confident, how would you behave?

You might say to yourself, "If I were more confident, I would stand up for myself. I would tell my harasser firmly to buzz off." All right, that's your goal. But begin with 10 percent more self-confidence. Begin by saying "no" directly to someone. "No, I can't lend you five dollars. I need it myself." "No, I can't take care of your baby while you go to the movies." Each time, say "no" firmly and politely. When saying no gets easier, say it to the harasser.

Do this for as long as it takes to try all ten qualities of your ideal self. If you want to be less sensitive to criticism, act 10 percent less sensitive to what other people say about you.

4. Give yourself credit for what makes you special. Every week, think of something you thought or did that you are proud of. Close your eyes and imagine how good you felt. Think about one of the good things that makes you special. Enjoy feeling special.

How to Reach Out

It may seem, from the outside, that strong people have it all together. But think about this: successful, happy people always have a *support system*. These winners have close, approving family

A close circle of friends help to make you feel better about yourself.

and friends. They have formed a larger network of helpers. They can exchange help and information with these people. Life is hard. These two support systems—a close circle of friends and a group of people you know—are most important to a happy, useful life.

All of the victims of sexual harassment we read
about—Sharon, Vanessa and Richie—became
isolated because of their problem. Sharon was the
only woman in the work group. She didn't have
any support on her job. Vanessa's problems grew.
She felt stupid and alone. Richie was afraid to
tell people about what happened to him. He was
afraid they would think it was his fault. Sexual
harassment often happens in secrecy. Because no
one knows about it, the harasser controls the
situation. That is why it is important to share the
problem with others. You must not let yourself
feel alone.

Strengthening your Intimate Circle

Most times, our family and friends love us. They
trust us and are on our side. We do not always
share our feelings with our parents. But we are
grateful when they understand. We want to talk
with friends about our problems. We want to tell
them that we are happy or sad or afraid.

We must talk about our life. We must share
feelings of love and comfort. We need to feel that
way to be happy. People are different from one
another. We will not see things the same way.
Nobody is perfect. But we need each other. So we
try to be there for each other. We help each other

when we feel angry, afraid, or frustrated about what is happening to us.

When you are having a bad time, you really need your friends. The best way to make good friends is to be a good friend. Follow the rule of "do unto others as you would have them do unto you." Here are some ways:

Listen. This is harder than you think. Let the other guy talk. Just listen and try to understand. Nod your head. Look at the other person. Don't start talking about your problems. Just be there for your friend.

Don't criticize. What we don't need when we are down is "I warned you." Don't say, "You always do this kind of thing." That won't help your friend.

Don't give advice. Try to help think of ways to deal with the problem. Help find several answers. Then let him or her choose.

Building a Network

A network is made up of people you know or look for who can help you. People at work can be your network. They may be willing to help. They may be the ones who pop in the back room when the harasser gets you there alone.

In schools, counselors and teachers are good people to contact. They are in the school at a different level. They know how things work. They may be the most helpful.

Churches have always been a great support. Churches are there to help people. They are a good place to go to get involved with other people. You can break out of being alone. It is the job of priests and pastors to listen and give advice.

Most cities have many support groups. Women's organizations have programs to help women with information and support. The National Organization for Women (NOW) has offices in many cities. You can call them about harassment. If they can't help, they may be able to tell you who to call.

Professional counseling is available, but it is expensive. You can call centers for self-help and self-development. These offer courses in things like learning to speak up for yourself, dealing with anger, and building self-esteem. You will get good information. And you will also meet other people with the same problems.

Becoming strong and sure of yourself will help you avoid harassment. Your power to handle yourself will show others that you are not a victim. With your new understanding of the problem maybe you can help others avoid harassment.

Glossary—*Explaining New Words*

authority   A person with the right or power to make things happen.

egotist   A self-centered, selfish person.

exploitation   Using a person for selfish purposes.

fantasist   Someone whose ideas of how to behave come from TV or movies.

grievance   A complaint.

harass   To disturb continuously. To cause a person to feel distress. To harm (someone) by repeated attacks.

harassment   The act of causing a person distress, or harming someone by repeated attacks.

harasser   A person who disturbs someone repeatedly.

hostile   Intended to hurt, unfriendly.

sadist   Someone who takes pleasure in causing pain.

stereotype   A very simple idea about a person or persons. It reduces the person to a few qualities.

vulnerable   Unprotected from danger, not well-defended.

Where to Go for Help

Equal Employment Opportunities Commission (EEOC)
1900 E Street, NW
Washington, D.C. 20415
(202) 632-6272

This government agency also has offices in major cities. Look in the telephone directory under United States Government.

Women Employed
5 South Wabash, Suite 415
Chicago, IL 60603

An organization to help working women. They publish a pamphlet on sexual harassment in the workplace.

National Organization for Women (NOW)
1401 New York Avenue, NW
Washington, D.C. 20005

Office of Civil Rights
200 Independence Avenue, SW
Washington, D.C. 20201

Women's Legal Defense Fund
200 P Street, NW
Washington, D.C. 20036
(202) 887-0364

National Legal Aid and Defense Association
1625 K Street, NW
8th floor
Washington, D.C. 20006
(202) 452-0620

For Further Reading

Adams, Virginia. "Jane Crow in the Army:
Obstacles to Sexual Integration." *Psychology
Today*, Vol 14, No. 5 (October 1980),
pp. 50–65. The author reports on sexual
discrimination and harassment of women in
the army. She reports on a study that claims
that 50 percent of the women interviewed said
they had been sexually harassed by a
supervisor. Women reported that sexual favors
were a way to get ahead.

Combatting Sexual Harassment. Women Employed
Institute, Chicago, IL, published 1983. This
pamphlet talks about the sexual harassment of
women in the workplace. It also includes
the EEOC guidelines for defining sexual
harassment, testimony given at a hearing, and
sample letters of complaint.

*Equal Employment Opportunity Commission: How to
    File Job-Related Sexual Harassment Complaints.*
    Working Woman's Institute, New York, New
    York, published 1983. Defines what is meant
    by sexual harassment as a violation of Title
    VII of the Civil Rights Act of 1964.

Lindsay, Karen. "Sexual Harassment on the Job
    and How To Stop It." *Ms. Magazine,* Vol 6,
    No. 5 (November 1977), pp. 47–51, 74,
    77–78. The author recounts instances of the
    sexual harassment suffered by women in
    nearly every occupation: clerical and
    factory workers, career women, waitresses,
    policewomen and actresses. She also indicates
    the alternatives open to victims.

United States Merit Systems Protection Board.
    *Sexual Harassment in the Federal Workplace: Is
    It a Problem?* Washington, D.C.: Government
    Printing Office, 1981. Twenty thousand
    government workers sent in questionnaires in
    the huge, nationwide study. The report
    examines the extent and impact of sexual
    harassment, its victims and offenders, and the
    awareness and perceived effectiveness of the
    remedies. Sexual harassment was found to be
    widespread.

Index

About the Author
Elizabeth Bouchard is a writer and a teacher in Chicago. She received
her Ph.D. from the University of Wisconsin/Madison, and is a professor
at Wright College, one of the City Colleges of Chicago. Dr. Bouchard
has also directed and produced theater, and reviewed plays for a local
radio station.

About the Editor
Evan Stark is a well-known sociologist, educator, and therapist
as well as a popular lecturer on women's and children's health issues.
Dr. Stark was the Henry Rutgers Fellow at Rutgers University, an as-
sociate at the Institution for Social and Policy Studies at Yale University, and a Fulbright Fellow at the University of Essex. He is the author
of many publications in the field of family relations and is the father of
four children.

Acknowledgments and Photo Credits
Photographs by Charles Waldron

Design/Production: Blackbirch Graphics, Inc.
Cover Photograph: Charles Waldron